More Than Just Words

Communication and Relationship Skills That Make a Difference

By
Brent D. Ruben, PhD and Watts Ruben

Getting an Early Start on Important Life Skills

A Book of Ideas, Situations, and Tools for Children and Their
Parents, Family Members, and Teachers to Read and Discuss Together

www.innovativeinkpublishing.com
Send all inquiries to:
4050 Westmark Drive
Dubuque, IA 52004-1840

Print ISBN: 9-798-7657-9022-9
Ebook ISBN: 9-798-7657-9023-6

Published in the United States of America

Table of Contents

Preface

Who Is the Book Written For?

More Than Just Words is written for young readers, but parents, grandparents, teachers, and other adults are encouraged to play an active role in discussing the material with their children. Doing so will provide an opportunity for more experienced readers to reflect upon and share their own approaches to communication and social relations and thereby to enhance learning by young readers.

Critical thinking about communication practices is an important developmental process at all ages. We all face an array of daily challenges and opportunities to become better communicators, and the material provided in this book is intended to be useful for encouraging reflection and learning to support this process at an early age.

The book is organized into two broad sections: The first introduces key communication ideas and tools, and the second presents a series of communication tips and mini "case studies"—hypothetical situations to which the ideas and tools discussed in Part 1 can be applied.

The mini case studies set up situations and ask readers what the characters in the short scenarios might be thinking and feeling, about various ways they might respond, and where these actions might lead. These scenarios and responses will provide opportunities for both younger and more advanced readers to talk about how the ideas presented in Part 1 apply in various situations, and to share their own approaches to communicating in these kinds of circumstances—and to explain why. These discussions provide an opportunity to talk through options, preferences, and the range of possible outcomes that may result from their choices. For example, some of the vignettes presented include comments of encouragement and support from one child to another that would likely be seen as helpful. Sometimes, however, there can be legitimate differences of opinion as to what the goal should be in a certain situation, whether comments or silence may be a preferred response, and whether the comments are best made in that moment or later, or in a public or private setting.

The goal of the book is to promote communication thinking and problem-solving—not to prescribe specific behaviors. The situations described do not come with textbook answers. Instead, they are designed as prompts for thoughtful reflections and conversations by children and adults in which various alternatives and outcomes can be explored.

Why Is the Content of This Book Important for Young Readers?

More Than Just Words introduces the concepts of communication and social relations. It presents ideas, skills, and tools that are important for successful and satisfying relationships, using language and examples to which children, their parents, and other older readers can easily relate.

We know that the benefits of being competent in communication begin when we are young and continue to be essential in personal, family, and professional activities throughout our lives. It is through communication that all activities with others occur. As critical as communication is to every facet of our lives, we may be quite unaware of the way communication works and how it influences us. Beginning with our earliest experiences—with parents, relatives, friends, electronic media, and other sources of information and entertainment—we are awash in a sea of messages. Though we generally don't think all that much about this, the messages that surround us provide lessons on a broad range of topics. They provide teachings that relate to how people express their values and opinions, understand and build relationships with others, participate in groups, collaborate and compete as a member of a team, and address the many challenging situations that we confront in our daily lives.

Not all the lessons provided for children are the ones we would choose. Despite our best efforts, there are many messages to which younger audiences are exposed that don't emphasize the importance of skills such as listening, empathy, collaboration, advocacy, creating healthy relationships, supporting others, and managing emotions and conflict constructively—all of which happen through communication. While these themes may be particularly helpful for children who are striving to improve their communication abilities, we must all be able to communicate with adults, make friends with peers, see things from others' points of view, and deal constructively with emotions.

The aim of this book is to focus attention on these and other vital aspects of communication and social interaction and to promote the development of helpful understandings and skills. Our intention is to highlight examples of how to apply this knowledge, and to do so in an informative and engaging way.

About the Authors

About the Authors

Dr. Brent Ruben is a parent and grandparent, and Distinguished Professor of Communication at Rutgers University. He is the author of *Communication & Human Behavior, Seventh Edition* (Kendall Hunt, 2020), and many other books about communication and leadership. Collaborator, Watts Ruben, is his granddaughter and an elementary school student in Cincinnati, Ohio.

The authors are grateful for input from a multi-generational team of family members and friends, which includes Jann Ruben, Larissa and Marc Ruben, and Robbi and Matt Urm, each of whom has provided encouragement and helpful suggestions as this project has progressed. We are also thankful to Karen Verde, for her editorial advice, and to Angela Lampe, Lynne Rogers, and Jennifer Wreisner from Innovative Ink Publishing for their guidance, support, and helpful suggestions

Introduction

Introduction for Young Readers

Learning to be a good communicator is important in so many ways. An understanding of communication and skills that help you to be successful and happy in your relationships with others is gained throughout your life. That learning begins when we are very young. You learn about communication from parents, siblings, friends, and from our many experiences. You also learn from books, television, and computers. This book, *More Than Just Words*, is written to highlight useful communication ideas and skills that will be essential when you are young and throughout your lives.

Part 1 of the book will explain what communication is and how it works. You will probably know some of these ideas already. After all, we communicate every time we talk. But as you will see, communication involves more than just talking, and we will discuss many other skills that are necessary for the communication process to work well in your daily activities, and help you develop great relationships with others.

Part 2 of the book describes a number of these helpful communication skills and offers communication tips. Each tip also comes with situations for you to think about and decide how you could apply your understanding of communication. We also want to encourage you to read and discuss the ideas and situations in the book with parents, teachers, relatives, siblings, or friends so that you can hear their thoughts on good ways to use communication.

We enjoyed working on this book, and we hope you will enjoy reading it. We also hope the ideas, skills, and tips will help you become an even better communicator than you are now!

Introduction for Other Readers

Communication and social skills are important to building and maintaining good relationships with family members, friends, peers, and acquaintances. Their contributions are underscored when we aspire to be valued and respected by others, when we are striving to be successful in achieving our aims or helping others achieve theirs, and when our communication competencies contribute to our own and others' satisfaction through our efforts. The important communication concepts and competencies that are needed through the course of our lifetimes are developed over many years, beginning with our earliest interactions with others and our exposure to computers, television, the Internet, print, texting, e-mail, social media, and video games. As parents, grandparents, guardians, and teachers, we do all we can to set good examples and to guide and monitor the experiences our children have in the world.

We know that, unfortunately, lessons taught from various sources may not support our values and ideals. We also know that not all the messages that children are exposed to are constructive or helpful.

More Than Just Words was written to help provide an early foundation for children related to valuable communication and relationship competencies. Part 1 of the book presents communication concepts in a way that is designed to be engaging and useful for young readers. Part 2 presents 10 tips and mini "case studies" to which the concepts from Part 1 apply.

In many respects, the content of the book parallels the content of university courses in communication and in interpersonal and social relations but presented in a simplified way and applied to provide a foundation—to provide a "head start on a college education," so to speak. The book encourages critical thinking, reflection, and skill development.

As discussed earlier, the benefits of this book will be most fully realized from dialogue between younger and more experienced readers. Many of the issues and tips provided will be familiar to adults, and discussions of the situations presented in Part 2 will provide an opportunity to explore alternative ways of handling these circumstances. A collaborative approach to using the book will also allow adults and children to share other communication challenges they confront and to discuss how best to handle these situations, as well as how the skills and tips presented in the book can help them to do so.

1 Understanding Communication

Communication: We Can't Get Along Without It

Communication is a part of life for all living things. People communicate with their pets. Birds communicate to fly in formation; ducklings engage in communication to follow their mother; and monkeys, dolphins, lightning bugs, and many other animals and insects communicate with one another.

As humans, communication is important to almost everything we do. It is the way we share ideas, information, and feelings.

Communication is also the way we …

•   Build relationships with family and friends

- Learn and solve problems

- Work together in groups and teams to get things done

- Help one another

Because it is such a big part of our lives, being as good at communication as we can is important—it can make a difference in our relationships with family and friends, how they feel about us, how we can get things done, and how we feel about ourselves.

Helping you to better understand communication and have great communication skills is the goal of this book!

How Communication Works

SENDING MESSAGES

Some of the most important messages are created through speaking and writing. This is what most people think of when they hear the word *communication*.

But for communication to take place, these messages must be seen or heard, and others must pay attention to them and make sense of them.

So, communication is not just about creating and sending messages for others, it's also about listening, paying attention to, and understanding the messages others are creating and sending to us.

- *What can happen if a message isn't created or sent in a clear way?*
- *What can happen if you don't listen carefully to a message someone sent your way?*

Nonverbal Messages. Spoken and written messages use words. But other messages do not use words. These are called *nonverbal messages*. The way we move our bodies and hands, the expressions on our faces, the way we move our eyes, and the way we dress and wear our hair are all ways of sending nonverbal messages.

Pictures and signals can also be ways of communicating. What do these pictures communicate?

Our own bodies are also sources of messages. Depending on the situations and people around us, these messages may be pleasurable, painful, or discomforting. Sometimes we think about the messages our body sends, sometimes we don't.

It can be very helpful to understand that our bodies can send messages that we should pay attention to. Knowing this helps us make good choices. What messages are these children here receiving from their bodies right now?

RECEIVING MESSAGES

For communication to work, messages must be sent, *and* they also must be received. Listening and seeing are the main ways messages are received, but smell, taste, and touch are other ways messages can be received. Looking at others and listening while they are speaking helps you understand their thoughts and feelings, and lets them know you are paying attention.

GETTING AND GIVING FEEDBACK

Feedback is a word used to refer to information that is "fed back" from a message receiver to a message sender. Feedback can be asked for by a sender—by asking a question after speaking, for instance. An example would be, "Does this idea make sense to you?" The answer is feedback. It helps a speaker know if more needs to be said or explained or if the receiver believes they have understood what the speaker wanted to communicate.

Feedback can also be nonverbal—nodding your head yes or no, or a facial expression, for example. Whether it is a spoken message or a nonverbal message, feedback can be very useful for improving communication. It is helpful to a speaker to know if—or how—he or she is being clear and understood. And it is helpful for a receiver because providing feedback gives them a chance to indicate if they are understanding a sender's messages or if they need to hear more. Feedback is also a way of letting others know if you agree or disagree with the messages you're hearing or seeing. And that can lead to helpful discussions.

TOOLS THAT HELP US COMMUNICATE

There are also tools—often called *communication media*—that we depend on to help with sending and receiving messages. Familiar examples are smart phones, e-mail, computers, television, texting, and social media. These tools give us more ways to communicate with people who are not in the same place we are. Some of tools also help us remember messages to use in the future, like phone messages, emails, or photos that we create or others send to us.

Communication goes on everywhere and all the time. All these settings have some things in common, yet all are different in some ways.

At home with family or at school …

In groups and on teams …

When you think about it, you realize that communication is happening every-where, all the time!!

How Can You Use These Ideas to Be a More Skillful Communicator?

In this part of the book, you will find 10 tips that you can apply to the ideas you read about in Part 1. Each tip also comes with one or more situations, and questions for you to think about. For each situation, think about how the ideas you read in Part 1 and the tips you read can be helpful. Think about the people in the situations and what you think they might say or do to apply the communication ideas, skills, and tips you have been reading about.

Every reader won't be interested in every one of these stories. Pick those that seem to fit you and your experiences best. Adults or older siblings can discuss these situations with you, tell you how they think about each situation, what they might do, and why. There is no one right or wrong answer for any of these stories. Different people might think and act differently depending on how they feel about the situation and their own approach to communication. Your main goal should be to read, think carefully about each story, and think about how best to handle each one. Also, think about how you could apply the tips and ideas in other situations with family, friends, and people you meet.

Tip 1: Be Clear, Truthful, and Accurate

When your messages are clear, truthful, and accurate, friends and family will learn to listen carefully to you and believe what you say. If your messages are often not clear or accurate, they may learn to pay less attention and may not always believe you.

Being honest, clear, and accurate is important for many reasons. It shows respect for others, lets others hear your thoughts and ideas, and helps them learn what matters to you.

When you are being honest, others may or may not agree with what you are thinking or saying. While honesty may lead to hurt feelings sometimes, it can also help create strong relationships and help others learn that there are many ways of thinking. Also, when people disagree it helps a person prepare for other situations in life. There will be many times when disagreements occur, and it is useful to develop good ways of listening to and learning from others when this happens.

If you disagree with others, try to listen respectfully before giving your opinion—to be sure you first understand what they are saying.

There may also be times when you decide not to share all your thoughts or feelings with others. If you think something you might say would be very hurtful, for example, it will be important to share your thoughts or feelings in a nice and respectful way, even though you disagree.

If you follow these tips, other people will also hopefully learn from what you are doing, and listen more carefully and respectfully when they share their feelings or thoughts with you.

Sometimes, it may be best to keep your opinions to yourself if they will not be helpful in any way. You may think about the situation, how you feel, what you believe is right, and what you might like to say. Deciding what to do or say in these situations can be difficult. You can then decide if it's better not to share your reactions—at least not right then.

There is a story about our first president, George Washington, that teaches some good lessons: "When Washington was six years old, he received a hatchet as a gift and when he was using it, he chopped down his father's cherry tree. When his father discovered the damaged tree, he became angry and asked George if he had done this.

Young George thought about what to say, and then was brave and said, "I cannot tell a lie… I did cut it with my hatchet." Washington's father thought for a moment and then hugged George and told him his being honest was very important and worth much more than the damage to the tree.

- *What did George's father most likely think when he first discovered the damaged tree?*
- *What was George probably feeling when his father asked him if he had chopped down the tree?*
- *Why do you think George told his father that he had chopped down the tree?*
- *When his father learned the truth, what did he want to communicate in his message to George?*
- *Why was this such an important message for his father to send to George?*

ANOTHER STORY TO THINK ABOUT

Your friend Jenny came to school with a new haircut that she tells you she really likes. Your first thought is that you don't think it looks that great.

- *What would you do in this situation?*
- *Would you share your thoughts with Jenny at this moment?*
- *Or would you keep them to yourself?*
- *Why would you make this choice?*
- *What might you be able to learn about communication and relationships from thinking about this situation?*

What do you think? What would you do?

Jen's mom asked her to walk to the grocery store to pick up some items she needed. She gave Jen money for the purchases. While walking around the store, Jen saw a bag of potato chips that looked tasty, and she thought they might be good to eat on the way home. Potato chips were not on her mom's list, but Jen decided to add these to her shopping basket anyway.

When Jen went to pay, she didn't have enough money. She put a container of milk that was on her mom's list back on the shelf, so that she had enough money to buy the chips.

When Jen got home, she handed her mom the bag and said she ran out of money so she couldn't buy the milk. Her mom looked at the groceries. She saw there was no milk, but she also saw an open bag of potato chips.

- *What do you think about Jen's choice at the store, and the story she told her mother?*
- *What might Jen have been feeling that led her to tell her mother the story about being short of money?*
- *What problems could Jen's story cause?*
- *If you were Jen, how would you explain what happened?*
- *Can you think of a situation when you had a hard time deciding whether to share your thinking or keep it to yourself? Why was it difficult to decide?*

Tip 2: Tune In to Nonverbal Messages

Nonverbal messages can give us clues about what people are feeling and thinking. When you or someone else is talking, it can be very helpful to watch their expressions and gestures to see what clues they may offer.

Nonverbal messages may help you know if others understand or are confused, or if they agree or disagree with what you or others are saying. Remember that nonverbal messages are clues, but we can also guess incorrectly about what they mean. Asking questions can help us figure out what nonverbal clues mean.

Jim asks Tina how she did at the soccer game. Tina doesn't say anything but looks down at the ground. Why do you think Tina might be looking at the ground?

- *What nonverbal clues would you be getting from Tina?*
- *Would you say or do anything if you were in Tina's place?*
- *What might you say next if you were in Jim's place after you saw Tina's reaction to your question?*
- *Why would you make these choices?*

You are with friends having lunch at school. You are laughing and having fun. Someone you know—but not very well—comes toward your table with their food tray and approaches an empty chair at your table. They stop for a minute and look at your table but then continue walking and sit down alone at the next table.

- *What are you thinking? What would you do?*
- *What are the nonverbal clues that might help you guess what the person is thinking?*
- *What might they be feeling?*
- *What could you do or say? Or would you not do or say anything?*
- *Why would you make that choice?*

Tip 3: Show Interest, Listen, Be Respectful

When people have thoughts or feelings they want to share, they appreciate it when others listen, are respectful, and make a sincere effort to understand the thoughts and feelings they are trying to express. Sometimes, it may seem like what you are hearing isn't really that interesting to you and it can be tempting to ignore or "zone out." In these moments, remember that listening carefully helps you stay connected to others. And by making an effort you will be able to learn more about other people and new things.

Listening is not always easy. To be a good listener you should pay close attention to what others are saying and let them know you are "tuned in" by your verbal and nonverbal messages. Try not to let your mind wander to other thoughts or think about what you want to say next. Remember that good listening is a skill that must be learned, and it takes practice to develop this skill.

Communication tends to work better when you are respectful of others and what they are saying. You show respect by what you say and how you say it, and by the kind of nonverbal messages you send. For example, looking at a person while they are talking shows respect, as does paying attention, by nodding to let them know you are actively listening and interested in what they are saying. Remember that paying attention, listening, and showing respect do not necessarily mean that you agree with all that you're hearing. They <u>do</u> mean that you are showing the courtesy of listening carefully and trying to be clear on what others have to say.

There is another reason to listen carefully, show interest, and be respectful. Remember how you feel when others don't pay attention to you or do not seem to be interested in what you have to say! It's not a good feeling! For many reasons, putting forth the effort to listen and try to understand is an important thing you can do to improve your communication skills and relationships.

WHAT DO YOU THINK? WHAT WOULD YOU DO?

Jamie is playing a video game when her grandmother, whom she hasn't seen for a long time, arrives for a visit. Of course, grandma is very anxious to see and talk with Jamie and other members of the family!

As she walks into the room where Jamie is, Grandma says "Hi, Jamie! It's great to see you! How are you doing?" Jamie is having a hard time looking away from the screen.

- *What is Jamie likely to be feeling and thinking?*
- *How might Grandma be feeling? Why?*
- *What do you think Jamie should say or do in this situation? Why?*
- *What might Grandma say or do to be helpful if she saw that Jamie was in the middle of doing something?*

Tip 4: Ask Questions

Asking questions can be very helpful for good communication. They are a way of asking for feedback, and the answers can provide information that will help improve clarity, accuracy, and understanding. Question asking also helps you get to know others better. If you are confused about what someone is saying to you, asking questions can help to clarify the message.

In addition to getting information, asking questions can make others feel good about you because they realize you are listening and taking an interest in them.

Closed-ended and open-ended questions. There are two kinds of questions: questions that can be answered with a yes or no, and questions that ask for more information. All questions are helpful, and sometimes, yes or no questions are perfect. They may be just what is needed to help the communication work well for the question asker or the question answerer.

Sometimes, though, yes or no questions are "communication enders." Once you say or hear yes or no, it can be hard to know what to say next. "Open-ended questions" don't have this problem, because they encourage others to share more information—rather than just answering with a yes or no.

An example of an open-ended question is, "What do you think about that?" A closed-ended question would be, "Did you like that?" Another open-ended question would be, "How do you feel?" and a closed-ended question would be, "Do you feel OK?"

Renee sits down next to you on the school bus. You have seen Renee in the hallways but never talked to her.

- *What could you do to start a conversation?*
- *What questions could you ask?*
- *Would a closed-ended or open-ended question be better in this situation? Why?*
- *What would be an example of a closed-ended question you could ask in this situation?*
- *What would be a good example of an open-ended question for this situation?*

Tip 5: Look for Opportunities to Talk with and Learn From Other People

You can gain a lot by talking with other people. You can learn about them and about their ideas and experiences.

When you talk with people who agree with you, their thoughts, feelings, and opinions can help you feel good about your own ideas. But it is also good to talk with and listen carefully to people who have different ideas, thoughts, and feelings so that you can learn about new or other ways of thinking about things.

When you talk with others who don't have the same opinions as you, what you hear might not change your mind. But it will give you something to think about—and remind you that people often think differently than you do, based on their own experiences.

A SITUATION TO THINK ABOUT

A good friend, Maria, has a cousin named Rick who is visiting from out of town. You have never met Rick before. You're invited over to meet him and spend the afternoon. When you arrive, Maria suggests that you all go for a walk. This is something you and Maria like to do, but her cousin Rick says he doesn't really like to walk. Then you suggest playing video games, which you and Maria also often enjoy. Rick says he doesn't like video games. Maria then suggests watching TV, but cousin Rick shakes his head no and says he doesn't think that's a good idea either.

- *What are your feelings at this point?*
- *What ideas do you have about what to say next?*
- *How might you go about making the most of the situation?*

Suppose you then decide to use your question-asking skills, and you ask Rick what he would like to do. He suggests the idea of creating a song or a dance. You and Maria don't know what to say because neither of you have ever done either of these things before.

- *What are you feeling about Rick's communication skills?*
- *What might you say at this point?*
- *What communication skills can you use to be helpful—like asking how it would work if you took turns doing what each person would most like to do?*
- *What can you learn from this situation, and how could you apply these skills in the future?*
- *Can you think of a time like this, where you were talking with someone who was not really agreeing with anything you suggested? What did you say and do? How did it work out?*

Your teacher asked you to draw a picture of something you really enjoy doing in the summer. You have a friend in the class named Fred. He shows you a picture he is working on, which he seems to be really proud of. You don't really like it, though. It seems strange to you. You can't really tell what it's even a picture of, and it doesn't seem like something Fred might do in the summer. He asks how you like his picture.

- *What are you thinking?*
- *What feelings do you have?*
- *What would you say?*
- *What communication skills could you use to make this a chance to learn something new?*
- *Can you think of other situations where you could use this skill?*
- *What lessons can be learned from this kind of situation?*

MISTAKES CAN BE LEARNING OPPORTUNITIES

If you make a mistake and others are offering comments or criticism, it can be hard to listen with an open mind. At first, we often get annoyed when this happens, and it is tempting to say we disagree or argue—either out loud or to ourselves. But it is good to become a person who can listen to criticism—even when it's hard to hear—and try to see it as a chance to learn lessons that can be helpful now and in the future.

WHAT DO YOU THINK? WHAT WOULD YOU DO?

After a baseball game, you are feeling bad because you struck out two times when you were at bat. After the game, your coach comes up to you and says there are a couple of things you were doing wrong when you were at bat. The coach tells you to be more careful about what pitches you swing at, and keep your eye on the ball.

- *What are your thoughts and feelings at this moment?*
- *What do you do or say?*
- *What communication skills can be helpful in this situation?*
- *What can you learn from this criticism that can help you when playing base-ball and in other situations where someone criticizes you?*

We also know that everyone makes mistakes now and then, and it's usually best to be honest with yourself and others when this happens. Sometimes you're not sure the criticism is correct or meant to be helpful. Even in these situations, it's good to listen and try to find ways to use the information you are receiving.

Other people like it when you can listen and think about what's being said, and this approach to communication gives you a chance to learn and do better in the future.

When you are offering a criticism or suggestions to others, keep in mind that picking a good time to share information contributes to good communication. Also, when your message is respectful and takes account of the others' feelings at the moment, it is more likely that the person you're talking to will pay attention and benefit from your suggestions.

You are at a party and you take pictures of others who are also there. Later you post the pictures on your social media account, and you get a text from one of your good friends who was not invited to the party. She didn't know about the party, so now she feels left out and asks why you didn't tell her about it and invite her too.

- *What is your friend likely thinking and feeling in this situation?*
- *What are your thoughts and feelings, and what might you say?*
- *Or would you choose to say nothing? How would you decide?*
- *Can you think of a situation like this in your life?*
- *How did you feel?*
- *What lessons can be learned from these kinds of situations?*

Tip 6: Take Turns Communicating

There are times when you are with your friends that you might have many ideas or feelings that you really want to share. In these situations, you probably find yourself talking a lot. At other times, you may not feel like saying much. Perhaps you're not too interested in the topic, are thinking about other things, or just don't have anything to add that you think would be appreciated or of interest to others.

It's helpful to keep in mind that, in most situations, it is a good idea to take turns when communicating—to be careful not to take too much of the "talk time" yourself, but also be sure to be an active communicator. Participating too much or too little can get in the way of good communication. Keep in mind that others will benefit from hearing what you are thinking, and you will benefit from hearing their ideas, too. This happens when everyone takes turns talking.

It's also helpful to remember that you and others will probably feel better if you all have a chance to participate in the conversation—talking but also listening. Taking turns in talking gives everyone the opportunity to contribute. But remember that everyone has their own approach to communication—some people are just more comfortable talking less, and some like to talk more. It's important to be aware and respectful of these kinds of differences.

You are with three friends and beginning to talk about what to do on Saturday, when you're getting together. One friend suggests, "It could be basketball or soccer. Both would be good."

He goes on to talk about how he really likes basketball more than soccer and shares a long list of reasons why that would be the best choice for Saturday. No one else has spoken or given any nonverbal clues about whether they agree or disagree. You realize that there hasn't been any "turn-taking"—and you or others haven't been able to share your opinions.

- *What feelings and thoughts do you have at this moment?*
- *What might you say or do when you realize that there hasn't been any turn-taking?*
- *What communication skills might be helpful in this situation?*
- *What lessons might be learned from this experience?*

Roni is sitting with friends and her friends are asking her questions about some things she would rather not talk about.

- *What feelings might Roni have?*
- *What might Roni be thinking?*
- *What could she say or do to make the conversation more comfortable for her?*
- *What communication skills might be helpful?*

Tip 7: Remember That Silence Communicates

Both verbal and nonverbal messages communicate. Silence can also communicate. Choosing to be silent can send a message. Exactly what the message is might not be clear, however. Sometimes, it's a way of saying you're thinking and not ready to speak. Sometimes it means you are not sure what you want to say, don't care about the topic, or are afraid others might not like your idea.

Whatever the reasons are, the message of silence can leave others wondering what you're thinking. That can be good or not so good, depending on the situation. You might be able to pick up on clues to what someone's silence means when you also pay attention to other nonverbal messages, like staring, frowning, smiling, or looking puzzled. And you can always ask questions to the person who isn't sharing their thoughts or feelings. The main point is to realize that silence, like talking, communicates, and you want to do what you can to be sure you are sending the messages you want to—and also that you are understanding what others are communicating if they are silent.

Alan is asking to copy your math homework since he hasn't finished his. You don't answer at first, and then Alan asks you the same question again and looks at you while waiting for an answer.

- *What are you thinking?*
- *Why might you not be answering?*
- *What could you do or say at this point?*
- *Why would you make this choice?*
- *What communication skills might be helpful in this situation?*

Tip 8: Think Before You Act, and Don't Let Your Feelings Control Your Communication

It's a good idea to think before you speak or act. This is especially true but also difficult to do when someone says something that you have a strong reaction to—maybe it is a criticism, teasing, or bullying.

It's usually best to pause and think about whether it's good to say something then, or to think and decide exactly what you want to say or do before answering. This is also true for e-mail, social media, or texting—even more—because the words and images that you post can be copied and sent to others—including some people you never even thought about when you posted. Try to be sure you are comfortable with anything you post on social media, because it will likely be around for others to see for a long time.

Jesse noticed a hurtful and rude social media post about a picture of her, and without giving the matter much thought, Jesse quickly responded with an insulting reply.

- *What thoughts and feelings was Jesse likely having?*
- *What was the problem with the first message?*
- *Was there also a problem with Jesse's response?*
- *What other ways might Jesse have handled this moment?*
- *What communication skills can be helpful in situations like this?*
- *If a situation like this came up in the future, what do you think you would do?*

We can have many different thoughts and feelings while we're speaking, listening, or watching others. Sometimes our feelings about what someone says or does will be strong. Especially when our reactions are negative, it is important to think about how others will react to your messages. Try not to let your emotions—especially anger or frustration—get in your way of paying attention, listening carefully, and responding in a clear helpful way, sending the message you really want to send.

Jonathan has been listening to Jake tell a very long story, and Jonathan is hoping Jake will stop talking soon because he must go to his next class, but Jake is going on … and on. Jonathan looked at his phone to check the time, thinking Jake might get the hint from his nonverbal message that he needs to get going, but Jake keeps talking.

- *What would your advice be to Jonathan about how to think about this situation?*
- *What would you do or say?*
- *Looking to the future, what might you do to help avoid a situation like this one from developing?*
- *Would it have helped if you let Jonathan know as he started talking, that you only had a few minutes because you were running to class?*
- *Could you have asked whether there was a good time to meet to talk later in the day?*

Tip 9: Be a Person Who Thinks About Others' Feelings

Being aware of and paying attention to others' feelings is very important for connecting and creating good relationships. To do this, you must listen carefully and watch nonverbal messages and imagine how you might feel in a situation if you were the other person.

Let others know that you are interested in and trying to understand their situation or feelings—whether they are happy, sad, frightened, or whatever. Sometimes it can be hard to know what to do or say. But it can be a wonderful skill to become a person who encourages and supports friends if they are having tough times, and who compliments others on their good feelings, happy times, and accomplishments.

Focusing on others' experiences and feelings takes effort. It is easy to pay so much attention to yourself and your own thoughts and feelings that you can forget how important it is to pay attention to others, by listening, trying to understand their feelings, and being caring and helpful whenever you can.

Mitsy, Caleb, and Jovi are discussing the idea of going for a swim. You are in the discussion too. You know that Mitsy and Caleb are good swimmers. And you're a good swimmer.

You know that Jovi does not know how to swim, but he is not telling the group that. You are waiting for him to say something, but he doesn't.

- *What might Jovi be thinking and feeling?*
- *What are your thoughts and feelings at this moment? What might you say to be helpful?*
- *Or would you choose to be silent?*
- *Why would you make this decision?*

Tony comes to school with new glasses that the eye doctor told him he needs to see clearly. This is his first day wearing them and he's trying to get used to the different feel and appearance. You are talking with him in the hallway when several other friends walk up and notice his different look, and one of the friends says, "Oh my gosh, you have glasses?!" and starts to laugh.

- *What might Tony be thinking?*
- *What are your thoughts and feelings?*
- *Are there things you could say to be helpful?*
- *Or would you choose to be silent?*
- *Why would you make this decision?*

Your good friend, Christine, calls to tell you that her grandmother is very sick, has just been taken to the hospital, and needs to have surgery. Christine seems upset and sad.

- *What are you thinking and feeling at this moment?*
- *What might you say?*
- *What communication skills could be helpful to you in this situation?*

Tip 10: Remember That Little Things Can Make a Big Difference

Remember that little things you say or do communicate a lot and can make a big difference to family members, friends, and people you meet. A few spoken words of thanks, or a text or e-mail on a birthday or special day, or a message of appreciation reminds others that you are thinking about them. It also sends a message that communicates you are the kind of person who is thankful for the part they play in your life. Even the simplest messages like "Hi," "How are you?" "Thanks," or "Excuse me" can create positive communication moments and help to make connections.

Even when no words are spoken, smiling and eye contact can be helpful in these moments. These nonverbal messages show friendliness, interest, and attention. There are, of course, situations where this may not be the message you want to send—for example, when looking too much at others can seem like staring and be upsetting to others, or where you don't want them to think you are overly interested in them or wondering what they may be doing. In general, however, even brief verbal or nonverbal messages can be very important to others, and bring you good feelings and a sense of satisfaction, as well.

WHAT DO YOU THINK ABOUT THE FOLLOWING SITUATIONS?

Waiting in Line at the Cafeteria

You are heading to the line at the school cafeteria. You get to the end of the line at just the same moment as a classmate, Ray. Ray smiles and says, "Hey, you can go first."

- *How does that make you think and feel about Ray?*
- *What might you say to him?*
- *Could what you do or say encourage Ray to do the same thing for someone else in the future?*
- *Can you think of other situations where a few words or a kind smile or gesture can be an important message that makes a big difference to others?*

A Surprise Meetup

Randall is walking on the sidewalk talking to his friend, Mark. He notices another friend, Rick—who he hasn't seen in a long time—walking up behind them. Randall remembers that Mark and Rick don't know each other.

- *What would Randall be thinking?*
- *What might Randall do and what might he say to his two friends?*
- *What might Rick be thinking as he walks toward them?*
- *What might Mark be thinking, and what could he say or do to help make this a positive communication moment?*

A Difficult Moment

Your grandparents drove from a nearby town to watch your soccer team play a game. Your team lost. You didn't think you played well, and you really don't feel like talking to anyone about the game right now. You're walking to the parking lot with your sister and grandparents.

- *What things might you be thinking about?*
- *What things might your grandparents be thinking about?*
- *What could you say as you all walk from the game toward the parking lot to try to make this a positive communication moment?*

Helping People You Don't Know

You are walking in the hallway at school and meet someone who is looking around and seems confused. You're very familiar with the school and know where things are.

- *What clues gave you the idea this person is lost and confused?*
- *What might be going through your mind and the other person's mind at this moment?*
- *Can you be sure you are guessing correctly about what the nonverbal clues mean? How can you check out your guess?*
- *Would you approach the person to talk? Why or why not?*
- *If you decide to approach them, what might you say?*

Final Things to Think About

The ideas, skills, and tips discussed in this book are meant to help you become a more effective and comfortable communicator—and to help others with whom you communicate to do the same. The situations offered in Part 2 are examples of times and places where you can use your understanding of communication to achieve a goal that you may have, to improve a situation, or strengthen your relationships. These are intended to be illustrations of the many situations when communication insight and skills can be extremely helpful.

There are no simple right or wrong answers as to exactly what to do or say in most situations. However, an understanding of communication and how it can help with social relations gives you tools that you can draw on in deciding what will be best for you in any particular setting.

A final point is that becoming skilled in communication, as becoming skilled in playing a sport or musical instrument, requires practice. The more one practices, thinks about how they did, and works to improve, the more skilled they become. This learning process starts when we are young, and it ideally continues throughout our lives as adults. We hope this book has provided a helpful introduction to this most essential life process.